THIS WALKER BOOK BELONGS TO:

_____

_____

_____

_____

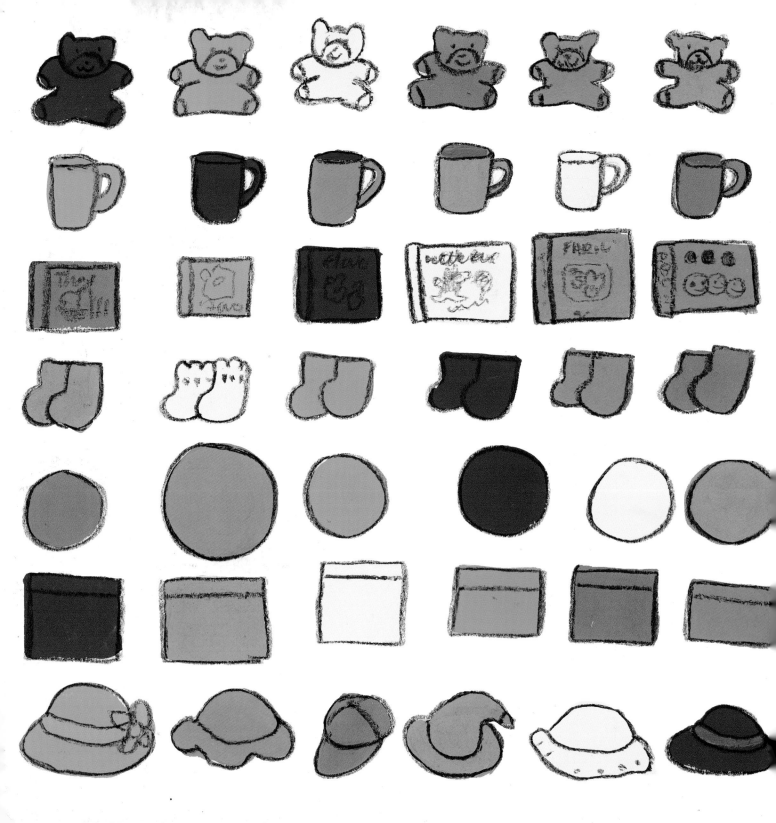

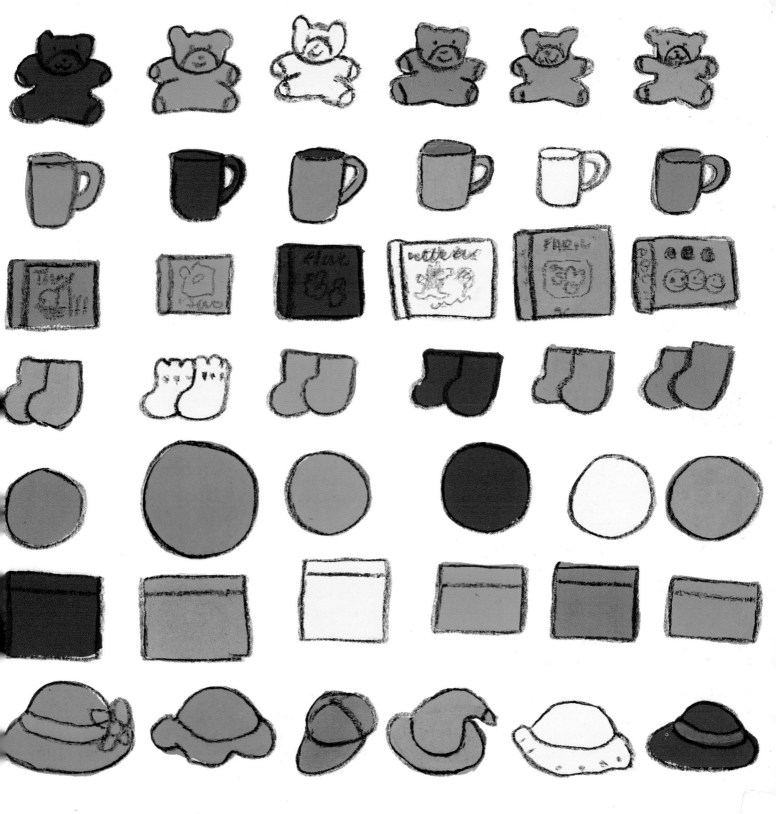

For my niece,
Lim Jia Ying
P. Y.

First published 1993 by Walker Books Ltd
87 Vauxhall Walk, London SE11 5HJ

This edition published 1998

2 4 6 8 10 9 7 5 3 1

Text © 1993 Richard James
Illustrations © 1993 Patrick Yee

Printed in Hong Kong

British Library Cataloguing in Publication Data
A catalogue record for this book is
available from the British Library.

ISBN 0-7445-6316-X

Colours for Katie

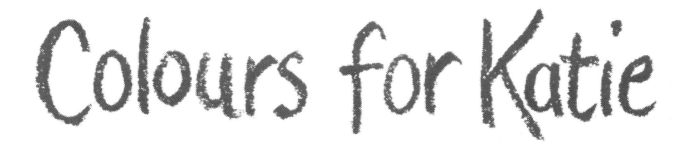

Written by Richard James
Illustrated by Patrick Yee

WALKER BOOKS
AND SUBSIDIARIES
LONDON • BOSTON • SYDNEY

Red socks and
green socks,
Brown socks
and blue,
Pink socks and
yellow socks too.
Which socks will
Katie choose?

The yellow socks.

Red hat and
green hat,
Brown hat
and blue,
Pink hat and
yellow hat too.
Which hat will
Katie wear?

The green hat.

Red ball and
green ball,
Brown ball
and blue,
Pink ball and
yellow ball too.
Which ball will
Katie play with?

The blue ball.

Red cup and
green cup,
Brown cup
and blue,
Pink cup and
yellow cup too.
Which cup will
Katie drink from?

The brown cup.

Red box and
green box,
Brown box
and blue,
Pink box and
yellow box too.
Which box will
Katie open?

The red box.

Red book and
green book,
Brown book
and blue,
Pink book and
yellow book too.
Which book will
Katie read?

The pink book.

Red bear and
green bear,
Brown bear
and blue,
Pink bear and
yellow bear too.
Which bear will
Katie cuddle?

All of them!

MORE WALKER PAPERBACKS
For You to Enjoy

TICKLE MONSTER
by Paul Rogers/Jo Burroughes

If you're ticklish, you'd better watch out – the Tickle Monster's about!
Where is he? Flip the flaps and see!

0-7445-6310-0   £3.99

WHAT DO I LOOK LIKE?
by Nick Sharratt

How do you look when you're having fun or feeling cross?
When you bang your thumb or get an ice-cream?
Flip the flaps and see!

0-7445-6311-9   £3.99

WHO'S ON THE FARM?
by Naomi Russell

Who's waiting by the gate? Who's rolling in the mud?
Who's splashing in the stream? Flip the flaps and see!

0-7445-6315-1   £3.99

WASHING LINE
by Jez Alborough

Whose are those enormous underpants, those stripy socks,
that tiny dress, hanging on the washing line?
Which animals do they belong to? Flip the flaps and see!

0-7445-6309-7   £3.99